Bibliographic information published by the German National Library:

The German National Library lists this publication in the National Bibliography; detailed bibliographic data are available on the Internet at http://dnb.dnb.de .

Imprint:

Copyright © 2017 GRIN Verlag, Open Publishing GmbH
Print and binding: Books on Demand GmbH, Norderstedt Germany
ISBN: 9783668540996

This book at GRIN:

http://www.grin.com/en/e-book/376004/international-relations-internationalization-strategy-of-the-body-shop

Anonym

International Relations. Internationalization Strategy of "The Body Shop"

GRIN Publishing

GRIN - Your knowledge has value

Since its foundation in 1998, GRIN has specialized in publishing academic texts by students, college teachers and other academics as e-book and printed book. The website www.grin.com is an ideal platform for presenting term papers, final papers, scientific essays, dissertations and specialist books.

Visit us on the internet:

http://www.grin.com/

http://www.facebook.com/grincom

http://www.twitter.com/grin_com

Internationalization Strategy of *The Body Shop*

30.12.2016

Title	Internationalization Strategy of *The Body Shop*
Degree Program	BWM - International Management
Module	International Relations

Table of contents

List of Abbreviations

f.	(and the) following (page)
ff.	(and the) following (pages)
FDI	Foreign Direct Investment
i.e.	id est / that is to say
e.g.	exempli gratia (for example)
OLI	Ownership-, Locational-, Internationalization- Advantages
EPRG	Ethno-, Poly-, Region-, Geocentrism
p	pence
p.	page
Plc	Public Limited Company
TBS	The Body Shop
Ibid.	ibidem (in the same place)
R&D	Research and Development
U.S.	United States
USA	United States of America
P&G	Procter & Gamble
CSR	Corporate Social Responsibility
U.K.	United Kingdom
SWOT	Strengths, Weaknesses, Opportunities, Threats
TBS	The Body Shop International Plc

List of Tables

List of Figures

1 Introduction

The Body Shop International Plc has been established in 1976 by Anita Roddick, as the first ethical beauty company to pioneer *"a new kind of sustainable business."*[1] Within a short period, it became a worldwide successful enterprise. Today, *The Body Shop* is a leader in the movement for creating an ethic of social responsibility among corporations and is one of the most controversial players within that movement. This essay describes the company's development, from opening the first shop, over its internationalization process, up to the acquisition by *L'Oréal.*

Therefore, some theoretical background in strategic international management will be explained. With the help of Porters Five Forces, changes within *The Body Shops* competitive environment will be discussed. By looking at the modes of entering foreign markets, as well as timing strategies, *The Body Shops* internationalization will be analyzed. Can the OLI-framework answer why the company has engaged in international markets in a certain way?

Especially after entering the U.S. market, the company faced some major challenges. The EPRG model will be applied, to see if those changed the way the company was managed. In 2005 *The Body Shop* went through a major repositioning, which ended up in the acquisition by *L'Oréal.* The latest part of this essay will describe the reasons and analyze the strategic position of The Body Shop before the takeover.

2 Theoretical Background

2.1 Strategic Management

Strategy is a series of measures adopted to achieve a stated aim.[2] *"Strategic positioning attempts to achieve sustainable competitive advantage by preserving what is distinctive about a company. It means performing different activities from rivals, or performing similar activities in different ways."*[3] Strategy in practice is an integrated concept for ensuring long-term survival, in active interaction with the competition, as well as the opportunities and threats within the company's

---

[1] Source: The Body Shop International Plc. (2015), p. 4
[2] Cf. Grattan, R. F. (2011), p 15ff.
[3] Source: Porter, M. E. (1996), p. 79

environment. Furthermore, a strategic concept is enabled in regards to the firm's individual strengths and weaknesses.[4]

Strategic Management is the process by which organizations determine that strategy, meaning their purpose, objectives and desired levels of attainment. It includes the decisions on actions for achieving these objectives, in an appropriate time-scale, and frequently in a changing environment, implement these actions, but also asses their progress and results.[5]

The mission and vision relate to the essential purpose of the organization and form the basis of its strategy. A mission describes what the company basically does. It provides an important tool for communicating ideals, as well as a sense of direction and purpose to internal and external stakeholders. Furthermore, it helps to guide the company's managers in resource allocation. The vision lays out the desired future state of the company and why the organization is existent. Values define how managers and employees should conduct themselves, how they should do business and what kind of organization they should build to achieve its mission.[6]

2.1.1 SWOT Analysis

To determine a strategy, its required to gather and analyze all necessary information. The SWOT analysis represents the basic analytical framework for strategy research. It breaks down the available information into four areas: Strengths, Weaknesses, Opportunities and Threats.[7]

Thus, a SWOT analysis sees the strategy of a company as the result of its (external or environmental) opportunities and threats, as well as its (internal) strengths and weaknesses. The SWOT analysis remains highly abstract in practice, as its findings are descriptive. It doesn't make any recommendations or sets any priorities.[8]

2.1.2 Competitive Forces

The job of a strategist is to understand and cope with competition. Very often managers define competition only by the rivalry among existing competitors,

---

[4] Cf. Kotler, P. et al. (2016), p. 11; Bickhoff, N. (2002), p. 53
[5] Cf. Ibid.; Thompson, J. / Martin, F. (2010), p. 11
[6] Cf. Hill, C. W. L. / Jones, G. R. (2012), p. 30ff.; Harrison, J. S. / St. John, C. H. (2009), p. 79
[7] Cf. Kotler, P. et al. (2016), p. 26ff.; Pahl, N. / Richter, A. (2007)
[8] Cf. Ibid.

which is to narrow. Porters framework includes four additional forces, that define an industries structure and shape the nature of competitive interaction:[9]

- Threat of Substitute Products or Services.
- Bargaining Power of Suppliers.
- Threat of New Entrants.
- Bargaining Power of Buyers.

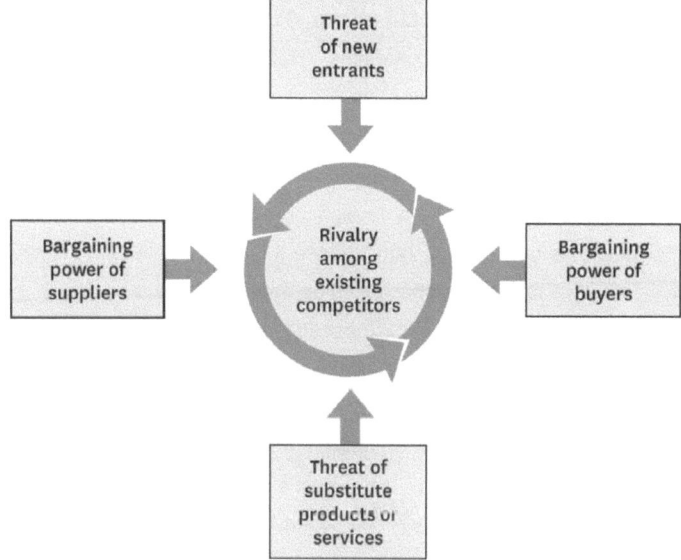

Figure 1: The Five Forces that shape Industry Competition[10]

If all five forces are intense, no company earns attractive returns on investment - if they are benign, many companies are profitable. Porters forces help to define a basis for a company's strategy, by giving a framework to analyze competitiveness within an industry. Based on that information, a company can structure and analyze its value chain, as well as its environment or potential market. Of course, the situation is always fluid, and the nature and relative power of forces will change, which makes it difficult to do a consolidated analysis.[11]

---

[9] Cf. Porter, M. E. (2008), p. 79f.
[10] Source: Porter, M. E. (2008), p. 79
[11] Cf. Porter, M. E. (2008), p. 79ff.; Thompson, J. / Martin, F. (2010), p. 113ff.; Kotler, P. et al. (2016), p. 39ff.

2.2 Internationalization Strategies

2.2.1 Eclectic Paradigm / OLI-Framework

The eclectic paradigm, also known as OLI-Framework, is a further development of the internationalization theory and has been published by John H. Dunning. It distinguishes between three forms of international activities: export, foreign direct investment (FDI) and licensing. The choice of any of these activities will be determined by the OLI-Factors. OLI stands for ownership-, locational- and internationalization advantages. These represent three potential sources of comparative advantages an Enterprise might consider, prior to becoming multinational. Ownership advantages address the question why some firms go abroad and describes firm-specific advantages, which allow to overcome the costs of operating in a foreign country. Location advantages focus on the question of where a firm choose to locate. Internationalization advantages influence how a firm chooses to operate in a foreign country.[12]

The OLI-frameworks key message is, that depending on the advantages a company holds and/or can achieve, it will choose its form of market entry mode. For example, if a business has ownership advantages only, it will choose licensing as its form of foreign market entry. If it has internationalization advantages additionally, it will start exporting. Only when locational advantages are possible, FDIs will be done. Following table summarizes the OLI-Framework's key-message.[13]

		Advantages		
		Ownership	Internationalization	Location
Form of market entry and foreign operation mode	FDI	x	x	x
	Export	x	x	-
	Licensing	x	-	-

Table 1: Market Entry and Market Cultivation Strategies in Dependence of the Advantage-Categories[14]

---

[12] Cf. Kutschker, M. / Schmid, S. (2011), p. 459ff.; Dunning, J. (1977), p. 395ff.; Neary, J. P. (viewed 07 December 2016), users.ox.ac.uk
[13] Cf. Ibid.
[14] Source: Kutschker, M. / Schmid, S. (2011), p. 459ff.

2.2.2 EPRG-Model

Heenans and Perlmutters EPRG-model is a framework to identify or determine a company's profile in terms of its international business strategy. The model states that a firm's senior management holds on four primary orientations when building and expanding its multinational capabilities. A company can be an:[15]

- ethnocentric-,
- polycentric-,
- region centric-,
- or geocentric organization.

An *ethnocentric* firm takes decisions based on what works within its home market, which can be described as *home country attitude*. *"This works at home; therefore, it must work in your country"*[16] is the leadership motto. Such companies test new ideas in the parent company's market, and transfer them to their subsidiaries. Export orders are viewed as additional sales. Decisions are made in the parent company and key management positions in subsidiaries are filled with managers from there.[17]

A *polycentric orientation*, also known as *host country orientation*, accepts significant differences between home and host countries. Positions in subsidiaries are filled by native mangers from the host country. Which are considered to act more compotont within that specific country. Decisions are made within the local subsidiaries, independent from the parent company.[18]

The *geocentric orientation*, or *world orientation*, sees the parent company and its subsidiaries as a worldwide unity. A geocentric company develops a specific character, which is independent from company's headquarters or individual countries cultures. Managers will be recruited irrespective of their nationality. Collective decisions will be made by the affected company's organizational units. A central point is the capability of resource allocation: instead of an independent procedure on a national perspective, the company establishes an international

---

[15] Cf. Kutschker, M. / Schmid, S. (2011), p. 287ff.; Heenan, D. A. / Perlmutter, H. V. (1979), p. 1ff.; Perlitz, M. / Schrank, R. (2013), p. 81ff,
[16] Source: Heenan, D. A. / Perlmutter, H. V. (1979), p. 12
[17] Cf. Kutschker, M. / Schmid, S. (2011), p. 287ff.; Heenan, D. A. / Perlmutter, H. V. (1979), p. 1ff.; Holtbrügge, D. / Welge, M. K. (2015), p. 48ff.;
[18] Ibid.

division of labor. It specializes its individual units on different tasks, to ensure competitive advantage.

The *region centric orientation* is a further development of the geocentric orientation. It's a reaction to the increasing regionalization of economies. Instead of looking at individual countries, it respects economic-areas, for example the European Union.[19]

The EPRG-model is giving a qualitative perspective on the internationalization process of a company. It focusses how a firm is managing its subsidiaries, i.e. the relationship between the parent company and its subsidiaries. The model reflects how a company's managements takes decisions, communicates, controls, and leads. However, its necessary to mention that no company executes a clear ethno-, poly-, region- or geocentric orientated. In fact, different approaches exist within different parts of a company.[20]

2.2.3 Global Timing Strategies

	Waterfall	Sprinkler
Advantages	- Resources do not all have to be provided at the same time. - Established markets can help to fund new markets by re-investing revenue. - Product life cycles might very in different regions and hence be extended. - Some markets can function as bridges for others. - Risks are limited if a market entry fails. - Initial Experiences help when entering other markets.	- Erects market barriers in several markets at the same time by setting standards. - Establishes a strong market position simultaneously, before followers or imitators can enter the markets or adapt to the services and products offered. - It may come as a surprise to customers and competitors at the same time. - Enables a faster amortization of fixed costs by economies of scale.

---

[19] Ibid.
[20] Ibid.

	Waterfall	Sprinkler
Disadvantages	- Losing time for entering other markets when a product is ready. - Attracting competitors as they can imitate the product and service. - Danger of lumping together different countries as lessons learned in one country are not necessarily helpful when entering others.	- The need for higher resources at a specific date. - Higher co-ordination efforts calling for special knowledge. - Danger of shortening life-cycles that ight result in consequently lower sales. - A higher risk of failure in several markets at the same time which would be potentially more damaging to the company. - The lack of 'lessons learned', that can help to improve market entries elsewhere.

Table 2: Comparison - Waterfall and Sprinkler Strategies[21]

Global Timing Strategies are necessary when a company wants to enter several foreign markets. It is possible to distinguish between waterfall and sprinkler strategies. By using the waterfall strategy, one market after the other is entered, which means the internationalization is increased step by step. When following a sprinkler strategy, the company bundles its resources to engage in all, or many markets, at the same time. A a mix of both strategies can also be applied, especially if the company has limited resources to fully execute a sprinkler strategy, but wants to take first-mover advantages in as many countries as possible. Upper table summarizes the advantages and disadvantages of both strategies.[22]

2.2.4 Country-specific timing strategies

	First-Mover	Follower
Advantage	- Gaining market knowledge. - Realizing cost advantages from economies of scale. - Gaining higher recognition as a pioneer. - Developing a strong brand and brand loyalty. - Setting standards. - Having a high market share.	- Possibility to learn from first mover failures. - Possibility to make use of a market that is already established (to a certain extend). - A given set of standards can be built on. - Information for own products and the market is already available. - Products and services of the first mover can be imitated and adjusted.

---

[21] Adopted from Kutschker, M. / Schmid, S. (2011), p. 985 ff.
[22] Cf. Kutschker, M. / Schmid, S. (2011), p. 989 ff.; Schmid, S. (2006), p. 20

	First-Mover	Follower
Disadvantages	- Higher costs for accessing the market. - Free-rider issues when followers make us of inventions of the first mover. - Entering markets with too much euphoria if the product is not evaluated objectively. - A higher risk of failure as there are no lessons to be learned from others.	- Followers must overcome possible market entry barriers. - Followers should even outrage the economies of scales of the first mover. - should break through existing networks of suppliers or customers. - Being trusted by customers is harder. - Equalizing the knowledge advantage of the first mover may proof hard.

Table 3: First-Mover vs. Follower[23]

When a company wants to gain competitive advantage, at least for some time, it can choose to be the first-mover abroad. Being a first-mover can have several advantages, for example the possibility to set higher market entry barriers for others. Followers can learn from first mover failures and use a market that is already established. Upper table summarizes the advantages and disadvantages of being a first-mover or follower.[24]

2.2.5 Modes of Entry

There are several ways for a company to engage in international business. The most common concepts are:[25]

- Licensing
- Export (direct / indirect)
- Mergers & Acquisitions
- Branch Offices
- Foreign Subsidiaries
- Representative Offices
- Joint Ventures & Strategic Alliances
- Distributors
- Agencies
- Marketing Representatives
- Franchising

---

[23] Adopted from Kutschker, M. / Schmid, S. (2011), p. 985 ff.; Johansson, J. K. (2003), p. 460f.;
[24] Cf. Kutschker, M. / Schmid, S. (2011), p. 985ff.; Johansson, J. K. (2003), p. 460f.
[25] Cf. Schmid, S. (2006), p. 14 ff.

As *The Body Shop* is known for their concept of working with franchisees, further explanations will be focused on that.[26]

2.2.6 Franchising

In franchising, many companies see an opportunity to expand their business model in a fast and efficient way.[27] The *European Franchise Foundation* defines franchising as follows:

"Franchising is a system of marketing goods and/or services and/or technology, which is based upon a close and ongoing collaboration between legally and financially separate and independent undertakings, the Franchisor and its individual Franchisees, whereby the Franchisor grants its individual Franchisee the right, and imposes the obligation, to conduct a business in accordance with the Franchisor's concept.

The right entitles and compels the individual Franchisee, in exchange for a direct or indirect financial consideration, to use the Franchisor's trade name, and/or trade mark and/or service mark, know-how, business and technical methods, procedural system, and other industrial and/or intellectual property rights, supported by continuing provision of commercial and technical assistance, within the framework and for the term of a written franchise agreement, concluded between parties for this purpose."[28]

That means, franchisee and franchisor are connected through a continuing obligation. The franchisor takes care about the further development of the system concept, as well as the active support and education of the franchisee. Therefore, the franchise invests isochronously and continuously pays dues to the franchisor. The main target of franchising is to ensure a homogenous customer perception. Internationally, several definitions of franchise systems can be found. However, a real franchise system must fulfill following characteristics:[29]

- System-related: Defines the vertical relationship between franchise and franchisor.

---

[20] Cf. Grass, H. (2011), p. 47, Schmid, S. / Daniel, A. (2006), p. 103ff.; Hodges, S. L. / Knaut, D. E. (1995), p. 108f.

[27] Ibid.

[28]Source: European Franchise Federation (viewed 04 December 2016), eff-franchise.com

[29] Cf. Grass, H. (2011), p. 10ff., Meffert, H. et al. (2015), p. 541ff.; Meurer, J. (1997), p. 9ff.;

- Contract-related: An individual, permanent, written contract defines the continuing obligation.
- Status-related: Legal and financial independence between both parties is given.
- Marketing-related: Franchising is a vertical sales system. An essential characteristic is the homogenous market appearance through standardization, e.g. of the shops, logos, branding etc.
- Functional-related: The tasks of the system partners are clearly defined, and usually differentiated by strategic tasks, fulfilled by the franchisor, and operative tasks, fulfilled by the franchise.

The benefits of franchising can clearly be seen in the speed at which expansion can take place, including global expansion.[30]

3 The Body Shop

3.1 History

In 1970, Anita Roddick visited "*The Body Shop*" housed in a car repairs garage in California, selling naturally scented cosmetic products. The shop used natural ingredients for its products and helped to employ and train immigrant women. Anita and Gordon Roddick founded a similar shop in the UK in 1976, using the same business name, color scheme and products (Roddick bought the exclusive rights to use "*The Body Shop*" name in 1992). The first franchise shop has been opened in 1977. One year later, the first overseas *Body Shop* was founded in Brussels. Since then, new shops opened by a rate of two per month.[31]

The Body Shop International Plc stock was floated on London's Unlisted Securities Market in April 1984, opening at 95 pence. It attained full listing on the London Stock Exchange in 1986. Until then, its price per share had raised to 820p. Within the next eight years the company's stock had split five times and its price rose about 10,944 percent.[32]

---

[30] Cf. Linstead, S. et al. (2009) p. 778
[31] Cf. Body Time (viewed 05 November 2016), bodytime.com; Bronstein, Z. (viewed 05 November 2016), berkeleydailyplanet.com; The Body Shop International Plc. (viewed 05 November 2016), thebodyshop.com
[32] Cf. Choi, D. Y. / Gray, E. R. (2011), p. 44 f.

In 2003 the company's share price went back down to 56.5p. London-based investment firm Investec Henderson Crosthwaite stated that *The Body Shop* is "barely profitable" on an ongoing basis. *"Their extraordinary expenses, reorganization charges, and costs of acquiring failing franchises have become recurring and commonplace."*[33] On 17th of March 2006, *The Body Shop* agreed to a £652.3 Million takeover by the French cosmetic firm L'Oréal (300p per share, while stock closing price has been 268p). L'Oréal stated that the company will continue to run independently from the UK. At that point, *The Body Shop* had 2,085 branches in 54 countries, 304 of them in the UK. Its total revenue in 2005 has been £415 million.[34]

Today, as part of the *L'Oréal* Group, the company runs 3102 Stores worldwide, of which 1134 are company-owned and 1,968 franchisees. 2015 Retail sales have been € 1559.6 million in total.[35] Following figure shows the company's sales split by regions.

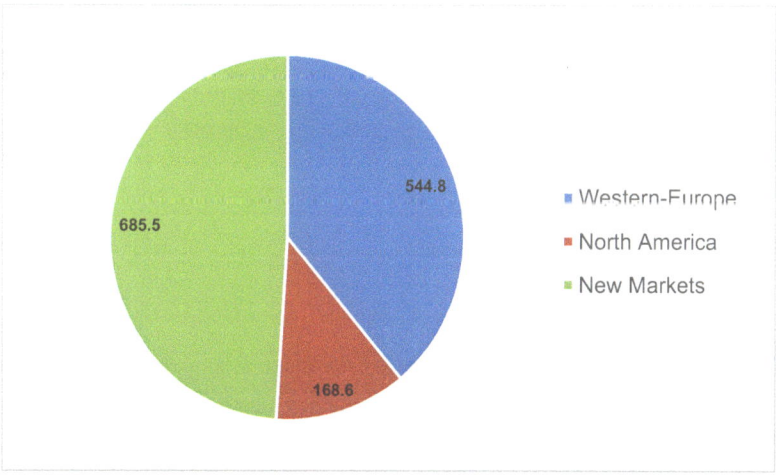

Figure 2: The Body Shop 2015 Retail Sales Split by Regions (Million Euros)[36]

---

[33] Entine, J. (viewed 04 December 2016), jonentine.com
[34] Cf. The Guardian (viewed 05 November 2016), theguardian.com
[35] Cf. L'Oreal (viewed 05 November 2016), loreal-finance.com
[36] Adopted from L'Oreal (viewed 05 November 2016), loreal-finance.com

3.2 Strategy

To get an idea of what the company differentiates from others, a closer look to *The Body Shops* strategy will be taken. As its mission the company states:[37]

"[...] Our Reason for being is to:

- *Dedicate our business to the pursuit of social and environmental change.*
- *Creatively balance the financial and human needs of our stakeholders: employees, customers, franchisees, suppliers and shareholders.*
- *Courageously ensure that our business is ecologically sustainable, meeting the needs of the present without compromising the future.*
- *Meaningfully contribute to local, national and international communities in which we trade by adopting a code of conduct which ensures care, honesty, fairness and respect.*
- *Passionately campaign for the protection of the environment, to defend human rights, and against animal testing within the cosmetics industry.*
- *Tirelessly work to narrow the gap between principle and practice, whilst making fun, passion and care part of our daily lives."*

To make sure, *The Body Shops* business continues to live by its mission statement, the company created five core values:[38]

- Support Community Fair Trade.
- Activate Self-Esteem.
- Defend Human Rights.
- Protect the Planet.
- Against Animal Testing.

The core values are being used as a practical guide to decision making at all management levels. Thus, the company runs a value-based strategy, which can bring the following benefits:[39]

- A better reputation among customers and other stakeholders, which improves the company's image and brings about new revenue sources.

---

[37] The Body Shop International Plc. (2009), p. 10
[38] Cf. The Body Shop International Plc. (2015), p. 4
[39] Cf. Ibid., Gong, Y. (2013), p. 90 ff.

- Employee satisfaction, morale, and retention, as well as stakeholder relations are improved. Furthermore, it opens new opportunities to collaborate, develop products, and keep stakeholders happy and confident.
- Long term sustainability, which improves economic value by reducing operating costs and optimizing lifecycle economic performance.
- It can help to conduct constructive dialogue with governments, regulators, local citizens, and pressure groups, which helps especially when a company relies on government permits.
- Inspires product, service, and market innovation as well as new business models or processes to achieve value-based competency.

In 2016, the company has unveiled its new 'Enrich not Exploit' strategy, which sets 14 specific, measurable targets. By that new CSR strategy, the company wants to further differentiate as a leader in sustainable business and organic cosmetic products. The strategy builds up on the five core values.[40]

3.3 Competitive Environment

By using Porters Five Forces framework, this part analyzes changes within the competitive environment of *The Body Shop* since its establishment. The key question is whether the competitiveness within the company's environment has gained or not. [41]

3.3.1 Threat of new Entrants

Incumbents like *L'Oréal, Nivea, Shiseido, Elizabeth Arden* and *Max Factor* have remarkably long staying power in the beauty industry. Most of these companies exist more than 100 years. Since the start of *The Body Shop* in 1978, many new entrants have emerged. Not only from the natural side, also luxury firms such as *Chanel, Dior, Ralph Lauren*, and *Yves St. Laurent* started to offer cosmetic products. Nowadays, two consumer goods giants, *Procter & Gamble* and *Unilever*, pose the most significant threats. As their traditional products mature, they increasingly pouring resources into their beauty divisions. But even if many new companies have entered the industry, incumbents managed to generate higher barriers during the last decades, especially for new companies that are

---

[40] Cf. Stustainable Brands (viewed 19 December 2016), sustainablebrands.com
[41] Cf. Porter, M. E. (2008), p. 79ff.; Thompson, J. / Martin, F. (2010), p. 113ff.; Kotler, P. et al. (2016), p. 39ff.

trying to upscale their business to a global level. For example, an unequal access to distribution channels is affecting the industry: Changes in consumer behavior, help no-frills retail chains such as *Wal-Mart* gain bargaining power, at the expense of fashionable department stores. *Wal-Mart* only wants to deal with a handful of big suppliers, which plays into the strength of incumbents like *L'Oréal* and *P&G*. It can be said that selling costs in department stores are much higher, while sales are declining. Furthermore, retail space, especially in the US market, is almost exclusively controlled by shopping malls, where most of the trading is done. Incumbents of the retail industry have a big advantage here, as they can rent a huge amount of shops at the same time. For example, *Bath & Body Works by Leslie Wexner*, who opened 100 stores within just 18 month after *The Body Shop* entered the U.S. market. A placement of a Bath& Body Works store in a mal usually precluded *The Body Shop* from entering the same mall. *TBS* focused on opening its shops in urban areas. Lately the company invested in innovating its shops designs, to differentiate the shopping experience specifically by adding more customer value, e.g. by offering beauty services, massages etc. [42]

3.3.2 Bargaining Power of Suppliers

The Body Shop grouped its environmental and social initiatives around the concept of product stewardship, entailing three dimensions:[43]

1. Products are examined under a life-cycle assessment scheme. Which offers a framework for comparing the quality of product materials and processes in terms of environmental protection and corporate social responsibility.
2. Since 1992 an environmental performance rating scheme has been in operation, which judges a supplier's performance with respect to legal compliance, environmental management systems, animal protection performance and any proactive initiatives the supplier takes.
3. *TBS* buyers receive guidelines and training to enable them to handle moral questions in purchasing.

Once a supplier meets *TBS's* environmental specifications, there is no pressure to achieve further improvements. Difficulties arise due to a tension between

---

[42] Cf. Preuss, L. (2005), p. 60f.; Roddick, A. (2005), p. 147ff.; Voigt, K.-I. et al. (2016), p.35; Carroll, A. B. / Buchholtz, A. K. (2015), p. 583
[43] Cf. Preuss, L. (2005), p. 60f.

environmental requirements and purchase price, which is evident for the supply base. Environmental initiatives undertaken for *The Body Shop* offer limited potential for gaining business elsewhere. Among new potential customers, only large companies show interest in the environment-friendly products, but even these wouldn't pay a price premium. Especially suppliers from the chemical sector commented that the volume of *TBS* was too small to attempt to influence their own suppliers. Clear limits to environmental initiatives in *The Body Shop's* supply chain thus emerge from financial constraints. However, the company is perceived to be an environmental leader, with only few competitors demonstrating a similar level of attention to the environment. For the supply chain, there is little incentive outside *The Body Shop* purchases, to address environmental issues. It can be summarized that, even if the competition within the economic beauty (or organic cosmetic products) industry gained extremely, the demand for raw materials fulfilling a high level of environmental standards, did not increase significantly. This can be led back to the fact that most of *The Body Shops* new competitors, focus their business on profits, instead of fulfilling certain economic values. Suppliers are still not dependent enough on *The Body Shops* revenue to adopt their standards. *The Body Shop* tries to gain bargaining power by providing a minimum of 12-month estimates of the quantities needed and carrying out a mid-year review, to ensure that production is on track and meets the targets. That means, the company provides suppliers with detailed forecast information for its upcoming demand, which exceeds industry norms.[44]

One of *The Body Shops* core values is to engage in fair trade. Therefore, the company is sourcing natural ingredients, e.g. from Nanhu Indian woman in Mexico, Kaypo Indians in Brazil etc. *TBS* seeks out small-scale farmers, traditional artisans, rural co-ops etc., and establishes fair trade partnerships with them. It helps these groups, which mainly come from development-countries, to start and develop their own business and income. Besides, *The Body Shop* gains more independency from large suppliers.[45]

---

[44] Cf. Preuss, L. (2005), p. 60f.; Thorpe, J. / Fennell, S. (2012), p. 13; Roddick, A. (2005), p. 147ff.; Voigt, K.-I. et al. (2016), p. 35
[45] Cf. Robbins, P. T. (2001), p. 96ff.

3.3.3 Bargaining Power of Buyers

The bargaining power of buyers in the industry is low. However, it has been mentioned before, that the industry has faced major changes in customer behavior during the last years. For example, a rising number of customers prefer to shop in no-frill retail chains. Furthermore, people don't differentiate between companies, which are using the economic approach just for marketing reasons, and those that are establishing real economic values within the value chain. *The Body Shop* struggled from that and had to focus on a better differentiation of its activities and products, which will be further described within the next part. That shows that customers don't face any switching costs or hesitate to switch brands at any time. However, market research firm *Grand View Research* states that the global market for organic personal care is about to grow significantly to a $25.11 billion a year in 2025. The interest in organic health care is obviously growing, which gives *The Body Shop* a good foundation for the future to gain revenue.[46]

3.3.4 Threat of Substitute Products or Services

Incumbents try to emphasize how unique their products are persistently. *L'Oréal* for example, advertised how many patents it has filed. *Shiseido* claimed that its *Body Creator* skin gel can helps to lose body fat. In the early years of the company, *The Body Shop* has been differentiated from other beauty companies by its core values, standing for a sustainable business and organic beauty products. *TBS* sold products with a hype-free presentation, reflecting values, that set the company apart from its competitors. The 'profit with principles' philosophy differentiated the company from its competitors. In the 70s and 80s. most cosmetic brands had identities based on glamorous user imagery and powerful functional, emotional, and self-expressive benefits, supported by dramatic packaging and advertising. *The Body Shop* clearly benefited from being a first-mover in pioneering an ethical approach within the beauty industry.[47]

However, the company couldn't construct the barriers it needed, to protect the market for ethical beauty products for itself, particularly in the United States. After entering the U.S. market in the late 80s, more and more competitors copied *The*

---

[46] Cf. Roddick, A. (2005), p. 147ff.; Assenmacher, K. (2011), p. 9 f.; Voigt, K.-I. et al. (2016), p. 35; Research, G. V. (viewed 10 December 2016), grandviewresearch.com; Preuss, L. (2005), p. 60f.; Wappler, C. (2006), p. 58
[47] Cf. Ibid.; Aaker, D. A. (2010), p. 108

Body Shops concept without sticking to its core values. Customers didn't differentiated copies from the original and didn't emphasize *The Body Shops* environmental activities. Especially since the beginning of the 21st century, *TBS* started to work more innovating its products and marketing. Today, the company is focusing on skin care and launched a new premium product line. This, as well as organic beauty products and sustainability are expected to be major trends within the beauty industry in the next decade.[48]

3.3.5 Rivalry Among Existing Competitors

Earlier explanations already indicate, that the competitive environment of *The Body Shop* has gained massively. Around 30 new direct competitors started to offer similar product lines and concepts as *The Body Shop*, just within a few years after the company entered the U.S. market. It has been mentioned before that only two years after entering the U.S. market in 1988, *The Body Shops* product concept has been copied by *Leslie Wexners Bath & Body Works*. Within 18 months *Wexner* had 100 stores grossing a revenue of $45 million per year. Today its an aggressive competitor with three times the revenue of *The Body Shop* in 2014, and three times higher operating profit margins – yet without a comparable social commitment. Another example is *Lush*, who started its business as a supplier of *The Body Shop*. *Lush* has now become an example of good practice, because of its innovate and holistic approach to sustainability. The company is engaged in projects that go far beyond those related to cosmetics, like campaigning against detention without trial or torture. *Lush* produces cosmetics without any packaging at all, which is very innovative and provides them with a sustainable advantage. The development of smart products reduces the production, transport and storing of bottles or pots. Moreover, these products do not require any preservatives, save a large amount of water and produce less waste, which saves production costs.[49]

TBS reacted to the increasing number of competitors by further differentiation: They opened shops in urban areas and adopted a micro-market approach, as

---

[48] Cf. Kono, T. / Lynn, L. (2007), p. 215; L'Oréal (2016), p. 38f., Assenmacher, K. (2011), p. 9 f.; Roddick, A. (2005), p. 147ff.; Voigt, K.-I. et al. (2016), p.35; Research, G. V. (viewed 10 December 2016), grandviewresearch.com; Łopaciuk, A. / Łoboda, M. (viewed 18 December 2016), toknowpress.net

[49] Cf. Assenmacher, K. (2011), p. 9f.; Lush (viewed 26 November 2016), lush.com

well as dual language stores - e.g. Spanish and English in California or Japanese and English in Hawaii.[50]

The emerging competitors pose both: a threat and an opportunity. The threat is that they will take away business from *The Body Shop*. However, the opportunity is, that their marketing activity will stimulate greater numbers of consumers to use natural cosmetics, which can already be seen in the expected market trends by *Grand View Research*. Thus, boosting *The Body Shop's* performance too, because of their market reputation. However, it can be summarized that *The Body Shop* had experienced a lot of problems, due to the massive growing competitiveness, especially during the 90s and the beginning of the 21st century. The next parts of this essay will describe some of them in detail.[51]

3.4 Internationalization Strategy

The Body Shops internationalization started two years after it has been founded, by opening the first shop in Brussels. Today, the company runs over 3000 shops in more than 60 countries. This part describes the company's internationalization strategy. Therefore, it will look at the timing and entry modes, *The Body Shop* applied. The company experienced major challenges, especially when entering the U.S. market, which will be analyzed in detail. The OLI-framework and EPRG-model will be applied, to see if they can answer why *The Body Shop* made certain decisions during its internationalization and if they can constitute certain challenges, the company has been confronted with.

3.4.1 Timing

Year of opening	Country
1976	UK
1978	Belgium
1979	Austria, Greece, Sweden
1980	Iceland, Canada
1981	Denmark, Ireland, Finland
1982	France, Netherlands
1983	Cyprus, Germany, Switzerland, Singapore, Australia
1984	Italy, Hong Kong, Malaysia
1985	Norway, Bahamas, Bahrain
1986	Portugal, Spain, Kuwait, Oman
1987	Malta, Antigua, Bermuda, Qatar, Saudi Arabia
1988	Gibraltar, United States, Taiwan
1989	Cayman Islands, New Zealand

[50] Cf. Roddick, A. (2005), p. 147ff.; Voigt, K.-I. et al. (2016), p.35
[51] Cf. Hodges, S. L. / Knaut, D. E. (1995), p. 113; Wilson, P. / Bates, S. (2004), p. 37; Łopaciuk, A. / Łoboda, M. (viewed 18 December 2016), toknowpress.net

Year of opening	Country
1990	Indonesia, Japan
1991	Luxembourg
1993	Mexico, Brunei, Thailand, Macau
1996	Philippines
1997	Korea
1999	Romania
2006	India
2014	Brazil
2016	Marocco, China, Sri Lanka

Table 4: International Expansion of The Body Shop[52]

Upper table shows the international expansion of *The Body Shop International Plc*. The company engages in new international markets by applying a waterfall strategy. This can be led back to the limited resources available in the company's early years. Furthermore, finding the right partners, who are willing to stick to the company's core values, has also been challenging. Through its franchise concept *The Body Shop* can expand quickly in existing markets. New marketing- and product ideas will be tested in the U.K. first and later introduced to other countries. In terms of pioneering the ethical approach to the global beauty industry, *The Body Shop* is clearly a first-mover. However, the company hasn't been able to generate entry barriers, to avoid followers from gain a significant market-share, particularly in the U.S. Followers benefit from the experiences *The Body Shop* gives them, by adopting the organic or ethical approach.[53]

3.4.2 Modes of Entry (applying the OLI-paradigm)

The Body Shops values and strategy, as well as its knowledge in sourcing natural products, can clearly represent the company's ownership advantages:[54]

- Value-based strategy concept and company's philosophy with five core values.
- Product know-how and creativity.
- Creative research and development.
- Supply chain management
- Quality management.
- Marketing and customer retention.

---

[52] Adopted from The Body Shop International Plc. (1999); L'Oréal (2016); L'Oréal (2014)
[53] Cf. Wilson, P. / Bates, S. (2004), p. 37; Johansson, J. K. (2003), p. 460; Kutschker, M. / Schmid, S. (2011), p. 985 ff.; Assenmacher, K. (2011), p. 9 f.; Roddick, A. (2005), p. 147ff.; Voigt, K.-I. et al. (2016), p.35; Schmid, S. / Daniel, A. (2006), p. 103ff.
[54] Cf. Kutschker, M. / Schmid, S. (2011); p. 460ff.; Holtbrügge, D. / Welge, M. K. (2015) p. 80ff.; Voigt, K.-I. et al. (2016), p. 29ff.

- Exotic, valuable ingredients.

The earlier mentioned characteristics of franchise systems can also be adopted to *The Body Shop*:[55]

- System-related: *The Body Shop* deals with head-franchisers, who are licensed to sub-franchise with the owners of the retail outlets. In some cases, the head franchiser also assembles products under license.[56]
- Contract-related: *TBS* franchise define the financial and legal relation, as well as the franchisors commitment to the company's values.
- Status-related: Legal and financial independence between both parties is given.
- Marketing-related: All *Body Shops* look similar, use the same marketing and products to ensure a homogenous image.
- Functional-related: All strategic decisions, as well as the product development, marketing activities and core values are defined by *The Body Shop International Plc*. The franchisees are outlets, focusing on sales and micro-environmental marketing activities, which stick to pre-defined core values.

Its franchise system allows *TBS* to expand quickly in existing markets. Due to its knowledge in ethical manufacturing and sourcing, but also to ensure the products are made in regards to the core values, the company used to manufacture in Littlehampton and export products worldwide. The production know-how involved can clearly be an internationalization advantage, which underlines the validity of the OLI-paradigm. In the early 2000s the Littlehampton factory has been sold and production completely outsourced. The reason has been the massively gaining competition, which put *TBS* under pressure to realize higher margins.[57]

Meanwhile the company uses a mixed strategy: while franchisees help to quickly expand in existing and new markets, *TBS* also opens company-owned department stores. Reasons for that can be found in better margins, as well as in optimizing the image by having a better control of the selling point, more flexibility and speed. E.g. by acquiring a majority stake in *Emporio Body Store* (51%

---

[55] Cf. Grass, H. (2011), p. 10ff., Meffert, H. et al. (2015), p. 541 ff.; Meurer, J. (1997), p. 9ff.
[56] Cf. Quarter, J. (2000), p. 120
[57] Cf. Kutschker, M. / Schmid, S. (2011); p. 460ff.; Holtbrügge, D. / Welge, M. K. (2015) p. 80ff.; Thompson, J. / Martin, F. (2010), p. 332; Choi, D. Y. / Gray, E. R. (2011), p. 28ff.; Baker, L. (viewed 11 December 2016), independent.co.uk (lately the company stopped manufacturing and focused on establishing a supply network instead)

shares), which has 130 franchisees, *The Body Shop* entered the Brazil market lately. Brazil, offers a platform for additional growth, as it's the fourth largest beauty market in the world.[58]

3.4.3 Challenges in the U.S.-market

The Body Shop had more than 200 shops in 33 countries before opening the first one in the United States. Roddick tried to gain experiences about the North American market through expanding to Canada, eight years before finally opening the first store in the US in 1988. After launching some more company-owned shops, the first franchisees were licensed. Until 1993 around 125 *Body Shops* opened, of which 94 have been owned by franchisees. The company's total revenue at this point has been £37.8 Mio. with a profit of £2.1 Mio. However, between 1993 and 2000 revenue stagnated and the company started to generate losses. In the beginning of 2005 only ten of the 313 *Body Shops* within the US have been owned by franchisees (for comparison: 70% of the international shops have been franchised). There have been several reasons for the bad reputation in the U.S.:[59]

- As mentioned before, after entering the U.S. market, *The Body Shop* experienced a massively gaining number of direct competitors copying their concept, e.g. *Bath & Body Works*. *The Body Shop*, at that point, didn't have a strategy to cope with competition. Roddick states: *"We had not thought of what might happen if a big retailer like Wexner, who rents an enormous amount of retail space in the malls in America, suddenly decided to turn one unit in each mall into a copycat of the Body Shop. Immediately, we had 500 shops competing with us. We never even thought like that. We imagined people could separate the authentic from the imitation, the real from the frivolous. But in America that kind of discernment was absolutely irrelevant."*[60]

- While *Roddick* strongly produced in compliance with the company's ethical principles, the competition followed an aggressive expansion strategy. They

---

[58] Cf. Schmid, S. / Daniel, A. (2006), p. 103; Annual Report 2011 p. 65; L'Oréal (2014), p. 70f.; Wappler, C. (2006), p. 3ff.; Hodges, S. L. / Knaut, D. E. (1995), p. 108; Carroll, A. B. / Buchholtz, A. K. (2015), p. 583

[59] Cf. Roddick, A. (1991), p. 147ff.; Schmid, S. / Daniel, A. (2006), p. 104ff.; Grass, H. (2011), p. 48ff.; Voigt, K.-I. et al. (2016), p.35; Grimond, M. (viewed 9 December 2016), independent.co.uk; Piercy, N. F. (1999), p. 225ff.

[60] Source: Roddick, A. (2005), p. 147

tried to copy the natural image of the *Body Shop* but didn't orientate to the same values. E.g. *The Body Shop* couldn't use about 50% of the ingredients because they had been tested on animals, while the competition did. Thus, purchase prices have been massively more expensive for *TBS*.

- *The Body Shop* didn't adjust to the cultural related preferences of US customers. However, the local competition used their market knowledge to actively serve the customer needs:

  o Shop personal of *The Body Shop* was directed to let customers unoffended, which contradicts the U.S. mentality: Customer service in the U.S. is identified by sales personal that follows the customer by every step through the store, to help or answer possible questions.

  o While the competition offered discounts, *The Body Shop* kept a strict price policy without any rebates. This has been related to the short margins the company earned, due to its franchise concept with three margin levels, as well as the high purchase prices mentioned before.

  o In the mid-90s *The Body Shop* started to send out their catalogues and take direct orders from final customers. Franchise became less attractive, as Franchisees saw the company as their own competition.

  o Franchisees felt disadvantaged compared to the company owned stores especially in terms of delivery times. There have been several court cases between franchisees and *The Body Shop International Plc.*[61]

  o Products haven't been adopted to the references and needs in overseas markets.[62]

In 1996 The Body Shop's U.S. operation lost £3.4 Million. Gordon and Anita Roddick stepped back from their executive positions and Patrick Gournay became the new company's CEO. He announced a plan to position *The Body Shop* as a powerful retailer (without any manufacturing facilities). The plan included:[63]

---

[61] Cf. Adler, C. (viewed 07 December 2016), archive.fortune.com
[62] Cf. Piercy, N. F. (1999), p. 223
[63] Cf. The Body Shop International Plc. (1999), p. 23f.; Roddick, A. (2005), p. 164f.; Palmer, A. (2012), p. 35; Funding Universe (viewed 09 December 2016), fundinguniverse.com; Piercy, N. F. (1999), p. 224ff.

- To decentralize the company's management into four main geographical areas: United Kingdom, North America, Asia, Europe.
- Looking for new manufacturing partners per region, to produce products closer to the market and more appropriate to local market requirements.
- Close or sell factories to make the company a true retailing company instead of a vertically integrated manufacturing business and wholesaler (the company owned factories have only been running at 30 per cent capacity during that time).
- Increasing the number of company-owned shops, rather than franchisees.
- A plan to open between 50 and 60 new company-owned shops per year.
- Improve the new products time-to-market.
- Continue to redesign the shops.

Due to positive feedback from business analysts, the company's share rose immediately after Gournays plans have been announced. Anita Roddick continued to work on new products and shop design, while Gordon Roddick focused on the franchise part of operations.[64]

3.4.4 Identifying The Body Shops Leadership Conception (applying the EPRG-model)

The previous part described the problems *The Body Shop* experienced when entering the U.S. market. The main reason can clearly be seen in the strategic leadership, development and control, which came from the parent company, more precisely, from its founder Anita Roddick herself. It has been developed in the U.K. and not adopted to the U.S. or other regions. In other words: the subsidiaries within specific regions haven't been given the authority to adopt *The Body Shops* standards to their local market. A clear *ethnocentric assumption* by the company's senior management can be seen here. Thus, *The Body Shops* venture to the U.S. market has been an unprofitable until the company started restructuring in 1999. Within Gournays new plan, clear tendencies to a more region centric approach could be seen. The decentralization of the management

---

[64] Ibid.

and manufacturing of products to specific regions, helps to adopt to local market requirements.[65]

3.5 Reasons for the companies repositioning in 2005

The early 2000s have been tumultuous for *The Body Shop*. The company continued to grow, while sales and profits stagnated. Even in the UK, the company found itself in a much more competitive marketplace. The Roddicks began to look for someone to buy the company, but talks collapsed due to the low price they could achieve for the company.[66]

In 2001 Franchisees raised lawsuits against *TBS*, because they felt disadvantaged compared to the company owned shops. Owners complained that the company-owned stores had no product availability problems, while franchisees had to wait month for deliveries.[67]

Anita and Gordon Roddick, stepped down from their positions as co-chairs of the board of directors in 2002. Together with their friend, and early investor Ian McGlinn, they maintained control of more than 50% of the company's voting rights. Anita Roddick remained to be involved in a consultant role. The first discussions with potential buyers began but where abandoned, when the offers under the company's expectations. The former North American CEO, Peter Saunders, was promoted as the global CEO to replace Patrick Gournay. Saunders strategic priorities were tighter cost controls and new products.[68]

In 2003 the company's share price went down to 56.5p. London-based investment firm *Investec Henderson Crosthwaite* stated that *The Body Shop* is "barely profitable" on an ongoing basis. "Their extraordinary expenses, reorganization charges, and costs of acquiring failing franchises have become recurring and commonplace." However, the company could already increase profits for the first time since years in the first half of 2003. Ongoing improvements

---

[65] Cf. Grass, H. (2011), p.49f.; Mueller, B. (2006), p. 107; Holtbrügge, D. / Welge, M. K. (2015), p. 48ff.; Kutschker, M. / Schmid, S. (2011), p. 287ff.; Heenan, D. A. / Perlmutter, H. V. (1979), p. 1ff.; Perlitz, M. / Schrank, R. (2013), p. 81 ff.; Roome, N. J. (1998), p.142ff.; Wilson, P. / Bates, S. (2004), p. 37
[66] Cf. Carroll, A. B. / Buchholtz, A. K. (2015), p. 589; Marsh, H. (viewed 7 December 2016), campaignlive.co.uk
[67] Cf. Adler, C. (viewed 07 December 2016), archive.fortune.com; Entine, J. (viewed 04 December 2016), jonentine.com
[68] Cf. Carroll, A. B. / Buchholtz, A. K. (2015), p. 589;

in new product development, marketing and supply chain have been the reasons for that.[69]

While the company could boost sales through new product releases and store designs, operating profit fell around 9 per cent in 2005. Lower than expected Christmas trading in 2005 led share prices to tumble 20 per cent back in January 2006. Though, the company could increase sales in the 2005 financial year. Following SWOT-analysis summarizes strengths, weaknesses, opportunities and threats of *The Body Shop International Plc* in 2005. [70]

3.5.1 Strength

- Company is still growing.[71]
- One of the world's best-known brands and the only global brand to set out on environmental and social issues.[72]
- The Body Shops values are more contemporary compared to when the company started.[73]
- New global campaigns: With Greenpeace for environmental sustainability; and against violence in homes led to better reputation.[74]
- Experience in Specialty Stores, Franchise Concepts and Direct Business Models.[75]
- Manufacturing plant sale allows focusing on optimizing retail business management.[76]

3.5.2 Weaknesses

- Littlehampton based plant leads to high manufacturing and distribution costs.[77]

---

[69] Cf. Entine, J. (viewed 04 December 2016), jonentine.com; William Reed Business Media SAS (viewed 18 December 2016), cosmeticsdesign.com

[70] Cf. Pitman, S. (viewed 18 December 2016), cosmeticsdesign.com; Pitman, S. (viewed 18 December 2016), cosmeticsdesign.com; Pitman, S. (viewed 18 December 2016), cosmeticsdesign.com

[71] Cf. Marsh, H. (viewed 7 December 2016), campaignlive.co.uk

[72] Ibid.

[73] Ibid.

[74] Cf. Carroll, A. B. / Buchholtz, A. K. (2015), p. 589

[75] Cornelissen, J. (2011), p. 158

[76] Cf. Baker, L. (viewed 11 December 2016), independent.co.uk

[77] Cf. Roddick, A. (2005), p. 267 f.

- Three layers of margin (The Body shop wholesales to the head franchisee, which then wholesaled to the sub franchisee) leads to even higher product costs[78]
- Getting a new product into market took the company more than six month.[79]
- 10% of all US stores are run by franchisees in comparison to 70% of all worldwide stores. Franchising within the US seems to be unattractive.[80]
- Sales and Profits stagnating.[81]
- Limited management structure to match the challenges it faces with over 1800 shops in 49 markets.[82]
- Outdated shop design.[83]
- High R&D and Marketing costs.[84]
- Missing resources for new product development and marketing innovation.[85]

3.5.3 Opportunities

- Outsourcing the productions can increase margins and
- High interest from incumbents in buying The Body Shop Company
- Growing interest in natural/organic brands at affordable price points in developed markets.[86]
- Opportunities for expansion in emerging markets.[87]
- High interest / demand from developing markets (e.g. China, Russia, India).[88]
- Growing market for organic beauty products, as well as companies that are considering economic sustainability.[89]

3.5.4 Threats

- Ethical standards on second- and third-party manufacturers need to be enforced.[90]

---

[78] Ibid.
[79] Ibid.
[80] Cf. Grass, H. (2011), p. 48 f.
[81] Cf. Mueller, B. (2006), p. 107; William Reed Business Media SAS (viewed 18 December 2016), cosmeticsdesign.com
[82] Cf. Marsh, H. (viewed 7 December 2016), campaignlive.co.uk
[83] Ibid.
[84] Cf. Wilson, P. / Bates, S. (2004), p. 37
[85] Cf. Palmer, A. (2012), p. 65
[86] Cf. Euromonitor International Ltd. (2012), p. 25
[87] Cf. Ibid. p. 26
[88] Cf. Wilson, P. / Bates, S. (2004), p. 37
[89] Cf. Ibid.
[90] Cf. Roddick, A. (2005), p. 267 f.

- Competition copies The Body Shop concept without sticking to its values, which makes them able to offer better pricing and special discounts.
- Much more competitive marketplace.[91]
- Barriers to entry for competitors are too low.[92]
- Franchisees filing Lawsuits against The Body Shop because they feel disadvantaged.[93]
- Strong Pound Exchange rate making the products seem rather pricey amid growing competition.[94]

L'Oréal became interested in the acquisition of The Body Shop as the takeover would provide the company a new perspective on retailing (specialty stores, direct-sales business), a brand capable of generating publicity in developing markets (China, Russia, India), an entry into the mass-market (premium mass cosmetics), a foothold in the Fair-Trade movement, and additional revenues.[95]

On the 17th of March 2006, The Body Shop agreed to a £652.3 Million takeover by L'Oréal (300p per share, closing price has been 268p). L'Oréal stated that the company will continue to run independently from the UK. The takeover met mixed reactions:[96]

4 Conclusion

By using Porters Five Forces Framework, the competitive environment of The Body Shop has been analyzed. The company experienced a massive gain in competitiveness. Since TBS entered the U.S. market, a high number of direct competitors emerged. Incumbents of the beauty industry started to generate higher entry barriers e.g. a limited access to retail space. Buyers don't hesitate to switch brands and don't emphasize with The Body Shops core values. Direct competitors offer higher discounts, due to the better margins they can generate by not having to stick on the same values as TBS, but still using the natural

---

[91] Cf. Marsh, H. (viewed 7 December 2016), campaignlive.co.uk; Euromonitor International Ltd. (2012), p. 25
[92] Kono, T. / Lynn, L. (2007), p. 215; Assenmacher, K. (2011), p. 9f.; Roddick, A. (2005), p. 147ff.; Voigt, K.-I. et al. (2016), p.35
[93] Cf. Adler, C. (viewed 07 December 2016), archive.fortune.com
[94] Cf. Ibid.; William Reed Business Media SAS (viewed 18 December 2016), cosmeticsdesign.com
[95] Cf. Cornelissen, J. (2011), p.158ff.
[96] Cf. The Guardian (viewed 05 November 2016), theguardian.com

cosmetics approach in marketing. *The Body Shops* bargaining power on suppliers isn't big enough to force those to comply their production with the company's core values, which direct influences *TBS* strategy. The company invested in obtaining from natives in development countries. That helps to increase the independency from big suppliers on one hand and realize the company's environmental approaches on the other.

The use of Porters five forces gave a very detailed impression of the competitive influences that were affecting *The Body Shops* environment. However, not all aspects of the model could be considered, due to limited availability of information. Furthermore, the framework is very detailed, other models like the PESTEL analysis may give a quicker overview and should be considered for future purposes.

The Body Shop engaged in new international markets by applying a waterfall strategy, especially because of its limited resources and to gain market experience. Due to its ownership advantages, meaning the company's strategy and knowledge to produce and sell products complying its core values, *TBS* choose franchising as its main form of entering and expanding in markets. The franchise model offered *TBS* to expand quickly with limited resources. Furthermore, the company has clearly been a first-mover in selling organic cosmetic products on a global level. It can clearly be said that *The Body Shop* created a new retail sector for natural cosmetic products.

As mentioned before, the company has been challenged by a major increase in competitiveness, which started after entering the U.S. market in the late 80s. Within a short period, the number of competitors offering organic beauty products gained massively. The EPRG model showed that *TBS* used a clear ethnocentric approach in its first period of internationalization. The company didn't adopt to any country or region specific preferences, which was a major reason for the problems within the USA. After Gournay took over the leadership, he started to transform the company to a more region centric orientation, by decentralizing its management and outsourcing its manufacturing. It can clearly be seen, that identifying and/or determining the right leadership model for a company strategic management can be a critical success factor.

However, even if Gournay put the company in the right direction, which can be seen by the increased share pricing, *TBS's* struggle continued in the early 2000's. Franchisees have been dissatisfied, competition extremely strong and the company's margins low. The need for a reinventing the company's products and marketing led to the company's sale. The *L'Oréal* takeover gave the company the opportunity to profit from the marketing and sourcing experiences of a global player, while staying independent and stick to its core values.

List of Literature

Aaker, D. A.: Building Strong Brands. 2nd Edition. Simon & Schuster. London 2010.

Adler, C.: The Disenfranchised. 2001.
http://archive.fortune.com/magazines/fortune/fortune_archive/2001/09/17/31026
3/index.htm
(viewed 07 December 2016).

Assenmacher, K.: The Body Shop - An Analysis of the Company's Actions towards Sustainability. 2011. Norderstedt: Anglia Ruskin University.

Baker, L.: Body Shop sells off manufacturing arm. 1999.
http://www.independent.co.uk/news/business/body-shop-sells-off-manufacturing-arm-1114818.html (viewed 11 December 2016).

Bickhoff, N.: Erfolgswirkungen strategischer Umweltmanagementmaßnahmen. 1st Edition. Springer-Gabler. Wiesbaden 2002.

Body Time: History. 2016. http://www.bodytime.com/about-us/history.html (viewed 05 November 2016).

Bronstein, Z.: Made In Berkeley: Berkeley's Body Time the Original Body Shop. 2016. http://www.berkeleydailyplanet.com/issue/2004-02-03/article/18201?headline=Made-In-Berkeley-Berkeley-s-Body-Time-the-Original-Body-Shop (viewed 05 November 2016).

Carroll, A. B. / Buchholtz, A. K.: Business & Society: Ethics, Sustainability, and Stakeholder Management. 9th Edition. Cengage Learning. Stamford 2015.

Choi, D. Y. / Gray, E. R.: Value-Centered Entrepreneurs and Their Companies. 1st Edition. Routledge. New York 2011.

Cornelissen, J.: Corporate Communication: A Guide to Theory and Practice. 3rd Edition. Sage Publications Inc. London 2011.

Dunning, J.: Trade, Location of Ecenomic Activity and the MNE: A Search for an Eclectic Approach. In: Ohlin, B.: The International Allocation of Economic Activity. 1st Edition. The Nobel Symposium. London 1977. p. 395 - 418.

Entine, J.: Body Shop's Packaging Starts to Unravel. 2002.
http://www.jonentine.com/reviews/Body_Shop_AFR.htm (viewed 04 December 2016).

Euromonitor International Ltd.: L'Oréal Company Profile - SWOT Analysis. Euromonitor International Ltd. London 2012.

European Franchise Federation: Franchising: definition & descriptions. 2016. http://www.eff-franchise.com/101/franchising-definition-description.html (viewed 04 December 2016).

Funding Universe: The Body Shop International plc History. 2003. http://www.fundinguniverse.com/company-histories/the-body-shop-international-plc-history/ (viewed 09 December 2016).

Gong, Y.: Global Operations Strategy: Fundamentals and Practice. 1st Edition. Springer-Verlag. Berlin 2013.

Grass, H.: Franchisesysteme im Zeichen der Globalisierung - Chancen und Risiken. 2011. Hamburg: FernUniversität Hagen.

Grattan, R. F.: Strategic Review - The Provess of Strategy Formulation in Complex Organisations. . 1st Edition. Gower Publishing Limited. Surrey 2011.

Grimond, M.: Body Shop has cultural problems. 1995. http://www.independent.co.uk/news/business/body-shop-has-cultural-problems-1618024.html (viewed 9 December 2016).

Harrison, J. S. / St. John, C. H.: Foundations in Strategic Management. 1st Edition. South-Western Cengage Learning. Mason 2009.

Heenan, D. A. / Perlmutter, H. V.: Multinational organization development : a social architectural perspective. 1st Edition. Addison-Weseley. Reading 1979.

Hill, C. W. L. / Jones, G. R.: Essentials of Strategic Management. 3rd Edition. Cengage-Learning. Mason 2012.

Hodges, S. L. / Knaut, D. E.: The Body Shop International. *In: Thomas, R. J.: New Product Success Stories: Lessons from Leading Innovators.* 1st Edition. John Wiley & Sons. New York 1995. p.

Holtbrügge, D. / Welge, M. K.: Internationales Management. Theorien, Funktionen, Fallstudien. 6th Edition. Schäffer-Poeschel Verlag. Stuttgart 2015.

Johansson, J. K.: Global Marketing: Research on Foreign Entry, Local Marketing, Global Management. *In: Weitz, B. / Wensley, R.: Handbook of Marketing.* 1st Edition. Sage. Thousand Oaks 2003. p. 457-483.

Kono, T. / Lynn, L.: Strategic New Product Development for the Global Economy. 1st Edition. Palgrave Macmillan. New York 2007.

Kotler, P. / Berger, R. / Bickhoff, N.: The Quintessence of Strategic Management. What You Really Need to Know to Survive in Business. 2nd Edition. Springer-Verlag. Berlin 2016.

Kutschker, M. / Schmid, S.: Internationales Management. 7th Edition. Oldenbourg. München 2011.

L'Oreal: L'Oréal Finance: The Body Shop. 2016. http://www.lorealfinance.com/eng/brands/the-body-shop (viewed 05 November 2016).

L'Oréal: Annual Report 2013. L'Oréal. Paris 2014.

L'Oréal: Annual Report 2015. L'Oréal. Paris 2016.

Linstead, S. / Fulop, L. / Lilley, S.: Management & Organization: A critical text. 2nd Edition. Palgrave Macmillan. Hampshire 2009.

Łopaciuk, A. / Łoboda, M.: GLOBAL BEAUTY INDUSTRY TRENDS IN THE 21st CENTURY. 2013. http://www.toknowpress.net/ISBN/978-961-6914-02-4/papers/ML13-365.pdf (viewed 18 December 2016).

Lush: A Lush Life. 2016. https://uk.lush.com/article/lush-life (viewed 26 November 2016).

Marsh, H.: BRAND HEALTH CHECK: THE BODY SHOP - Has The Body Shop lost its direction for good? 2001. http://www.campaignlive.co.uk/article/75110/brand-health-check-body-shop-body-shop-lost-its-direction-good-high-street-crowded-caring-retailers-body-shop-seems-lost-sight-its-brand-heritage#PJDEOALOw23dYTgu.99 (viewed 7 December 2016).

Meffert, H. / Baumann, C. / Kirchgeorg, M.: Marketing. Grundlagen marktorientierter Unternehmensführung. Konzepte - Instrumente - Praxisbeispiele. . 12. Auflage. Springer Fachmedien. Wiesbaden 2015.

Meurer, J.: Führung von Franchisesystemen. Führungstypen - Einflußfaktoren - Verhaltens und Erfolgswirkungen. 1st Edition. Gabler Verlag. Wiesbaden 1997.

Mueller, B.: Dynamics of International Advertising: Theoretical and Practical Perspectives. 1st Edition. Die Deutsche Bibliothek. New York 2006.

Neary, J. P.: Foreign Direct Investment: The OLI Framework. 2016. http://users.ox.ac.uk/~econ0211/papers/pdf/fdiprinceton.pdf (viewed 07 December 2016).

Pahl, N. / Richter, A.: SWOT Analysis. Idea, Methodology And A Practical Approach. 1st Edition
GRIN Verlag. Berlin 2007.

Palmer, A.: Introduction to Marketing: Theory and Practice. 3rd Edition. Oxford University Press. Oxford 2012.

Perlitz, M. / Schrank, R.: Internationales Management. 6th Edition. UVK Verlagsgesellschaft mbH. Konstanz 2013.

Piercy, N. F.: Tales from the Marketplace. 1st Edition. Routledge. New York 1999.

Pitman, S.: Exotic formulations boos Body Shop sales. 2005. http://www.cosmeticsdesign.com/Business-Financial/Exotic-formulations-boost-Body-Shop-sales (viewed 18 December 2016).

Pitman, S.: Body Shop owner defends selling to L'Oreal. 2006. http://www.cosmeticsdesign.com/Market-Trends/Body-Shop-owner-defends-selling-to-L-Oreal (viewed 18 December 2016).

Pitman, S.: Body Shop posts increased sales for 2005. 2006. http://www.cosmeticsdesign.com/Business-Financial/Body-Shop-posts-increased-sales-for-2005 (viewed 18 December 2016).

Porter, M. E.: What is Strategy? *In: Harvard Business Review.* 6. 1996, p. 61-78.

Porter, M. E.: The Five Forces That Shape Strategy. *In: Harvard Business Review.* 1. 2008, p. 78-93.

Preuss, L.: The Green Multiplier: A Study of Environmental Protection and the Supply Chain. 1st Edition. Palgrave Macmillan. Hampshire 2005.

Quarter, J.: Beyond the Bottom Line - Socially Innovative Business Owners. 1st Edition. Quorum Books. London 2000

Research, G. V.: Organic Personal Care Market Size To Reach USD 25.1 Billion By 2025. 2016. https://www.grandviewresearch.com/press-release/global-organic-personal-care-market (viewed 10 December 2016).

Robbins, P. T.: Greening the Corporation: Management Strategy and the Environmental Challenge. 1st Edition. Earthscan Publications Ltd. London 2001.

Roddick, A.: Body and Soul - Erfolgsrezept Öko-Ethik. 2nd Edition. ECON Verlag. Düsseldorf 1991.

Roddick, A.: Business as Unusual - My Entrepreneurial Journey. 2nd Edition. Anita Roddick Books. Chichester 2005.

Roome, N. J.: Sustainibility Strategies for the Industry: The Future of Corporate Practice. 1st Edition. Island Press. Waschington 1998.

Schmid, S.: Strategien der Internationalisierung - Ein Überblick. *In: Schmid, S.: Strategien der Internationalisierung - Fallstudien und Fallbeispiele.* 1st Edition. Oldenbourg. München 2006. p. 5 - 33.

Schmid, S. / Daniel, A.: Body Shop International - Schwierige Zeiten in den USA - erst recht für Franchisenehmer. *In: Schmid, S.: Strategien der Internationalisierung - Fallstudien und Fallbeispiele.* 1st Edition. Oldenbourg. München 2006. p. 103 - 110.

Stustainable Brands: The Body Shop Marks 40th Year with Pledge to Be World's Most Ethcal, Sustainable Global Company. 2016. http://www.sustainablebrands.com/news_and_views/brand_innovation/sustaina ble_brands/body_shop_marks_40th_year_pledge_be_worlds_most_e (viewed 19 December 2016).

The Body Shop International Plc.: Annual Report 1998. The Body Shop. 1999.

The Body Shop International Plc.: Living our Values. The Body Shop International Plc Values Report 2009. The Body Shop. 2009.

The Body Shop International Plc.: Building For The Future - Our Values Performance 2014/2015 & Our New Commitment. The Body Shop. 2015.

The Body Shop International Plc.: The Body Shop Heritage. 2016. https://www.thebodyshop.com/en-gb/heritage (viewed 05 November 2016).

The Guardian: L'Oréal buys Body Shop for £652m. 2006. https://www.theguardian.com/business/2006/mar/17/retail.money (viewed 05 November 2016).

Thompson, J. / Martin, F.: Strategic Management - Awareness & Change. 6th Edition. Cengage Learning EMEA. Hampshire 2010.

Thorpe, J. / Fennell, S.: Climate Change Risks and Supply Chain Responsibility. . 1st Edition. Oxfam. Oxfam 2012.

Voigt, K.-I. / Buliga, O. / Michl, K.: Business Model Pioneers: How Innovators Successfully Implement New Business Models. 1st Edition. Springer-Verlag. Basel 2016.

Wappler, C.: Comparative Analysis of Department Stores and Shopping Centers in Germany and Spain. 1st Edition. Diplomica Publishing GmbH. Hamburg 2006.

William Reed Business Media SAS: Profits hit the black for The Body Shop. 2003. http://www.cosmeticsdesign.com/Business-Financial/Profits-hit-the-black-for-The-Body-Shop (viewed 18 December 2016).

William Reed Business Media SAS: Disappointing 1Q for The Body Shop. 2004. http://www.cosmeticsdesign.com/Business-Financial/Disappointing-1Q-for-The-Body-Shop (viewed 18 December 2016).

Wilson, P. / Bates, S.: The Essential Guide to Managing Small Buiness Growth. 1st Edition. John Wiley & Sons. Chichester 2004.

YOUR KNOWLEDGE HAS VALUE

- We will publish your bachelor's and
  master's thesis, essays and papers

- Your own eBook and book -
  sold worldwide in all relevant shops

- Earn money with each sale

Upload your text at www.GRIN.com
and publish for free